The Quest

-FOR KIDS-

AN EXPEDITION TOWARD A DEEPER
RELATIONSHIP WITH GOD

OLDER KIDS ACTIVITY BOOK
BETH MOORE
WITH KATHY STRAWN
LIFEWAY PRESS®
NASHVILLE, TN

M000022249

© Copyright 2018 LifeWay Press®

No part of this work may be reproduced or transmitted in any form or by any means, electronic or mechanical, including photocopying and recording, or by any information storage or retrieval system, except as may be expressly permitted in writing by the publisher.

Requests for permission should be addressed in writing to
LifeWay Press®
One LifeWay Plaza
Nashville, TN 37234-0172

ISBN 9781535909600
Item 005804823

Dewey Decimal Classification Number: 268.432
Subject Heading: Discipleship—Curricula\God\Bible—Study
Dewey Decimal Classification Number: 248.82
Subject Heading: CHRISTIAN LIFE \ JESUS CHRIST—TEACHINGS

Printed in the United States of America
LifeWay Kids
LifeWay Resources
One LifeWay Plaza
Nashville, Tennessee 37234-0172

We believe the Bible has God for its author; salvation for its end; and truth, without any mixture of error, for its matter and that all Scripture is totally true and trustworthy. To review LifeWay's doctrinal guideline, please visit *lifeway.com/doctrinalguideline*.

All Scripture quotations are taken from the Christian Standard Bible

® Copyright 2017 by Holman Bible Publishers. Used by permission.

Table of Contents

MATTHEW 7:7-11

[8] FOR EVERYONE WHO ASKS **RECEIVES,** AND THE ONE WHO SEEKS **FINDS,** AND TO THE ONE WHO KNOCKS, THE DOOR WILL BE **OPENED.**

[7] **ASK,** AND IT WILL BE GIVEN TO YOU.

SEEK AND YOU WILL FIND.

KNOCK AND THE DOOR WILL BE OPENED TO YOU.

[9] WHO AMONG YOU, IF HIS SON ASKS HIM FOR **BREAD**, WILL GIVE HIM A A STONE?

[10] OR IF HE **ASKS** FOR A **FISH**, WILL GIVE HIM A **SNAKE?**

[11] IF YOU THEN, WHO ARE EVIL, KNOW HOW TO GIVE **GOOD GIFTS** TO YOUR CHILDREN, **HOW MUCH MORE** WILL YOUR FATHER IN HEAVEN GIVE GOOD THINGS TO THOSE WHO ASK HIM.

The Quest

GROWING CLOSER TO GOD IS OUR QUEST

*Quest – an act of seeking;
a search in order to find or get something*

THROUGHOUT THIS STUDY, WE WILL BE ON A QUEST TO GROW CLOSER TO GOD. THE BIBLE TELLS US GOD HAS ALSO BEEN ON A QUEST TO SAVE US AND BRING US CLOSER TO HIM.

GOD'S VERY GOOD PLAN

In the beginning, nothing existed except God. God went to work. He spoke and created light. He separated the water on earth from the water above the earth to make the sky. God made the dry land and the seas. He commanded the earth to grow plants and trees. He placed the sun, moon, and stars in the sky.

God created all living things in the water and all birds that fly. He added animals to cover the earth. God looked down at His creation and knew that it was good.

God created people. He made people special. God created people in His own image. God made a man, Adam, from dust of the ground. He breathed into the man, and the man became alive. God took a rib from the man and created a woman. Adam named his wife Eve.

God instructed the man and woman to care for the garden where He had placed them and to take care of the earth. God warned Adam and Eve: "You may eat of any tree in the garden except that you must not eat of the tree of knowledge of good and evil. If you eat of this tree, you will die."

The serpent questioned Eve. "Did God really say that you cannot eat of any tree in the garden?" he asked. Eve answered, "We can eat of any tree except the one in the middle of the garden. God told us we would die if we eat it or touch it." Satan lied, "No! You won't die. God just knows that if you eat the fruit, you will be like Him, knowing good and evil."

The fruit of the tree looked so good. Eve thought about being as wise as God. She took some of the fruit and ate it. She gave some to Adam to eat. He knew it was wrong to eat the fruit, but he ate it anyway.

Suddenly Adam and Eve realized they had no clothes on. They sewed leaves together to cover themselves. That evening, Adam and Eve heard God walking in the garden. They quickly hid themselves. God called to Adam, "Where are you?"

Adam answered, "I heard you in the garden. I was afraid since I have no clothes on. So I hid." God asked, "Who told you that you were naked? Did you eat of the tree I told you not to eat from?" Adam blamed Eve and God. "The woman You made for me gave me fruit and I ate it," he said. When God asked what she had done, Eve blamed the serpent. "The serpent tricked me," she said.

God punished the serpent. He punished Eve. He punished Adam. Yet, God also gave Adam and Eve hope. He promised that one day a descendant of Adam and Eve would crush the serpent. God clothed Adam and Eve in animal skins. God sent them from the garden.

—based on Genesis 1–3

RUN-AWAY ANIMAL TRACKS

Each animal track has an extra letter shown multiple times that doesn't belong. Find that letter (Hint: it always appears on the first print in the track) and cross it out. You will leave a trail that spells things from today's Bible story. Now, draw a line from each Bible word or phrase you've uncovered to the camping tent that describes it.

I AM THE ONE WHO DECEIVED THE WOMAN. I CAUSED HER TO THINK SHE COULD BE LIKE GOD!

I WAS A SPECIAL TREE IN GOD'S GARDEN. GOD TOLD THE PEOPLE NOT TO EAT MY FRUIT, BUT THEY DID IT ANYWAY.

I WAS TRICKED BY THE SERPENT, AND I DISOBEYED GOD.

GOD ASKED ME, "WHERE ARE YOU?" EVEN THOUGH HE KNEW WHERE I WAS.

ADAM AND EVE HID IN ME WHEN THEY REALIZED THEY HAD NO CLOTHES.

Now go back and find the letter you crossed out in each track. Write that letter in its corresponding circle to find a special word in this study. What is it and what does it mean?

QU PUZZLE

Fill in the crossword puzzle using the clues for words that begin with QU.

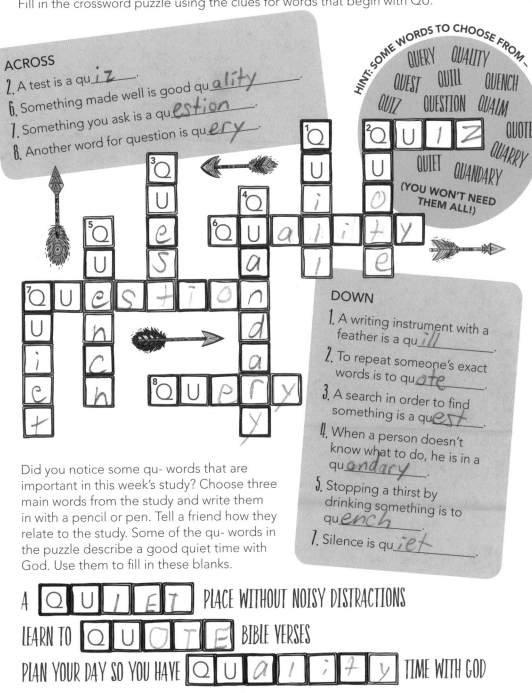

ACROSS

2. A test is a qu_iz_.
6. Something made well is good qu_ality_.
7. Something you ask is a qu_estion_.
8. Another word for question is qu_ery_.

HINT: SOME WORDS TO CHOOSE FROM –

QUERY   QUALITY
QUEST   QUILL   QUENCH
QUIZ   QUESTION   QUALM
QUOTE
QUARRY
QUIET   QUANDARY

(YOU WON'T NEED THEM ALL!)

DOWN

1. A writing instrument with a feather is a qu_ill_.
2. To repeat someone's exact words is to qu_ote_.
3. A search in order to find something is a qu_est_.
4. When a person doesn't know what to do, he is in a qu_andary_.
5. Stopping a thirst by drinking something is to qu_ench_.
7. Silence is qu_iet_.

Did you notice some qu- words that are important in this week's study? Choose three main words from the study and write them in with a pencil or pen. Tell a friend how they relate to the study. Some of the qu- words in the puzzle describe a good quiet time with God. Use them to fill in these blanks.

A ☐Q☐U☐I☐E☐T☐ PLACE WITHOUT NOISY DISTRACTIONS

LEARN TO ☐Q☐U☐O☐T☐E☐ BIBLE VERSES

PLAN YOUR DAY SO YOU HAVE ☐Q☐U☐a☐l☐i☐t☐y☐ TIME WITH GOD

QUERIES FOR THE QUEST

Query is another word for question. God asks us questions and listens to our questions to draw us closer to Him. These pages will guide you to use your Bible, to think about questions you have for God or ones He may have for you, and to journal your thoughts and feelings.

DAILY QUERY 1

➤ Read Genesis 1:26–2:17 and 3:1-9. What question did God ask Adam in Genesis 3:9? Write it here._____

➤ If you had to answer where you are now in your relationship with God, where would you say you are? Circle where you are on this scale and explain why you chose that number.

Far from God   Close to God
1   2   3   4   5   6   7   8   9   10

I chose this number because ... _____

DAILY QUERY 2

➤ Read Genesis 1:26-31

➤ One important question is "Who are You, Lord?" Write a few words here that Genesis 1:26-31 teaches about who God is.

_____   _____   _____

➤ Finish by ending this sentence: Lord, nobody but You is …

_____

DAILY QUERY 3

➤ Read Genesis 3:2-7. What was Eve seeking or looking for in this passage?

_____

➤ Sometimes we look for other things aside from what God has for us. Write a list of things you struggle with when trying to obey God.

➤ God, please help me to obey you when I am faced with … _____

DAILY QUERY 4

➤ Read Genesis 3:8-10. Write the question God asked Adam and Eve.

_____

➤ Write Adam's response to God- "I heard you in the garden and _____
_____ _____."

➤ Think about what makes you afraid. List some fears here: _____
_____

➤ Now read 2 Timothy 1:7. List the four things God has given believers to
use in fighting their fears.

1. _____ 2. _____ 3. _____ 4. _____

➤ Write about how these verses make you feel. Ask God any questions you
have about your fears and facing them. Thank God for the kind of help
you are most glad He gives.

_____

_____

DAILY QUERY 5

Assess Your Quest

➤ Look back at each day's query. Think about what you learned and whether
it changed how you think about God and growing closer to Him. Answer
each of the following questions:

➤ What truth did I discover this week?

_____

➤ What did I learn about myself and Jesus?

_____

➤ Is there anything I realized I need to confess to God and change?

_____

The Quest & Faith

FOLLOWING GOD'S PLAN

Search —

to look into or over carefully or thoroughly in an

effort to find or discover something.

GOD WANTS US TO SEARCH THE SCRIPTURES CAREFULLY
TO LEARN MORE ABOUT GOD AND HIS PLAN FOR US.

ABRAM'S JOURNEY

Abram lived with his wife, Sarai. One day, God called out to Abram. God had chosen Abram and told him to leave home and move to a place where he had never been. God promised Abram three things: a large family, land for his family, and blessing. Later, God visited Abram in a vision and said, "Do not be afraid, Abram. I am your shield; your reward will be very great."

God's promise was good, but Abram was sad because he didn't have any children to inherit his blessing. "One of my slaves will be my heir," Abram cried. But God's plan was boundless. He lead Abram outside to remind him of His promise. "Look at the sky and count the stars, if you can," God said. Abram couldn't count the stars. There were too many! "Your family will be that numerous," God promised. Abram believed God, and God was pleased.

God also promised that Abram's family would keep the land they were living in. Abram asked, "How can I be sure?" So God confirmed His covenant with Abram.

God told Abram to bring five animals: a cow, a goat, a ram, a turtledove, and a pigeon. Abram did as God said, and he divided the animals. Then, when the sun was setting, a deep sleep came over him.

While Abram slept, God told him what would happen in the future. He said that Abram's family would be slaves in another country for 400 years. After these 400 years, God would judge the nation and bless Abram's family. And God promised that in spite of all the difficult things that would happen, Abram would live a long and peaceful life.

After sunset, once it was dark, a smoking pot of fire and a flaming torch representing God passed between the divided animals. This sign demonstrated that God would be responsible for keeping His promise.

—based on Genesis 12:1-3 and Genesis 15:1-21

A QUEST FOR ANSWERS

Find and circle words from the Bible story (using the word bank) about Abram and Sarai in this word search. Recall how each word is used in the story.

WORD BANK

Abram
Abraham
children
covenant
descendants
God
grains of sand
impossible
Isaac
journey
land
laughter
Lot
Sarah
Sarai
son
stars
visitors

DIG DEEPER!

Read Genesis 17:1-8. Record God's words to Abraham.

God's Words	**What God Promised**
I will _____ you greatly. (17:2)	M __ __ T __ __ L __
I will confirm my _Covenant_ between me and you. (17:7)	C O V E N A N T
I will give you the _land_ where you are residing. (17:8)	L a n d

HAPPY CAMPERS

Someone has parked these campers in front of some important information about becoming a Christian. Can you fill in the missing letters to finish the statements? Hint: the missing letters are: POND   OD PRO   E SI   ULES

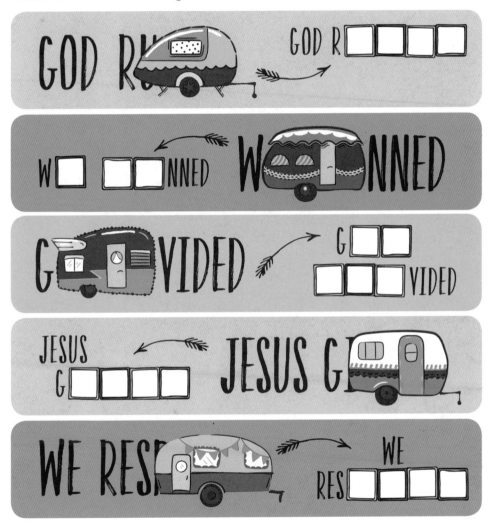

Draw a line from each of these statements below to the correct sentence above.
• God sent His Son, Jesus, to rescue us from the punishment of sin.
• God created everything.
• The Holy Spirit helps people know when to admit, believe, and confess to God.
• Jesus gave His life on the cross for our sin and then rose again.
• Everyone is separated from God because of disobedience.

QUERIES FOR THE QUEST

There are no right and wrong words for writing your thoughts and feelings. If you are concerned about putting them on paper, you can write in code or use initials to represent some words. Remember, these pages are for you and God only. If you miss a day, just begin the next time where you left off.

DAILY QUERY 1

Read Genesis 12:1-5.

➤ What truths do you notice about God in this passage?

_____

➤ What do you learn about who Abram is?

_____

➤ Name a time God asked you to obey, and you did.

_____

➤ Pray: Thank you, God, for helping me obey You …

_____

DAILY QUERY 2

Read Genesis 15:1-6.

➤ What do you notice about this passage that is different about the promises God made Abram in Genesis 12 from your Daily Query 1?

_____

➤ Write down what you see that God promised Abram in this passage.

_____

➤ How do you think Abram felt when God promised him these things?

_____

➤ Name one way you think God is asking you to obey Him.

_____

➤ Pray: Thank you, God, for your plan for me. Help me to follow it. These are places where I struggle to obey You sometimes …

_____

DAILY QUERY 3

Read Genesis 15:13-15.

➤ From this passage, we know God told Abram about how his family would become slaves in the future (we know they did later in Egypt). God promised He would take care of them, lead them out (we know Moses did this), and give them the land God has promised Abram. God even told Abraham that he would live a long life.

➤ Why do you think God told Abram these things?

_____

➤ What is one way you know you can trust God?

_____

➤ Pray: Lord, thank You that I can trust You for …

_____

DAILY QUERY 4

Read Genesis 18:9-14.

➤ What was so difficult in this passage for Abraham and Sarah to believe?

_____

➤ What is the answer to the question from this passage: "Is anything too hard for God?"

_____

➤ Pray, thanking God that He can do what seems impossible to others.

_____

DAILY QUERY 5

Assess Your Quest

➤ Look back at each day's query. Think about what you learned and whether it changed how you think about God and growing closer to Him. Answer each of the following questions:

➤ What truth did I discover this week?

_____

➤ What did I learn about myself and Jesus?

_____

➤ Is there anything I realized I need to confess to God and change?

_____

The Quest & Fear

TRUSTING AND DEPENDING ON GOD

Pursue — to find, to seek, to follow up

JESUS ACCOMPLISHED THE WORK OF SALVATION ON THE CROSS, BUT GOD PURSUES US TO HAVE A RESTORED RELATIONSHIP WITH HIM, JUST AS HE DID WITH ADAM AND EVE IN THE GARDEN.

JESUS CALMED THE STORM

Jesus spent all day teaching crowds of people near the Sea of Galilee. That evening, Jesus wanted to cross over to the other side of the sea. He said, "Let's cross over to the other side of the lake."

So Jesus and His disciples left the crowds. They got into a boat and began sailing. Some of the people from the crowds followed in their own boats. While Jesus and His disciples traveled, Jesus fell asleep on a cushion at the back of the boat.

All of a sudden, a storm came. The wind was strong, and the waves crashed into the boat. Water was coming into the boat, and the disciples were afraid! Many of the disciples were fishermen. They had survived storms on the sea before, but this storm was different. It was so strong. If the water kept coming in the boat, the boat would sink. Surely they would all drown!

The disciples looked to Jesus for help, but Jesus was still fast asleep at the back of the boat. He didn't seem to even notice the storm. Did Jesus care that they were about to sink into the sea?

The disciples woke up Jesus. "Lord, save us!" they said. "We are going to die!"

Jesus opened His eyes and saw that His friends were afraid. He got up and spoke to the wind. Then Jesus said to the sea, "Silence! Be still!"

At the sound of Jesus' voice, the wind stopped blowing and the waves stopped crashing. Everything was calm. The disciples were safe.

Jesus looked at His disciples and asked, "Why are you afraid? Do you still have no faith?" Did the disciples not trust Jesus to take care of them?

The disciples were amazed. "Who is this man?" they asked each other. "Even the wind and the waves obey Him!"

—based on Matthew 8:23-27; Mark 4:35-41; Luke 8:22-25

DRAW YOUR ANSWER

Read Luke 8:23-25 and put the Bible story in the correct order.

☐ **JESUS SPOKE TO THE STORM.**

1 **JESUS AND THE DISCIPLES GOT IN A BOAT.**

☐ **THE DISCIPLES WERE AMAZED THAT THE STORM OBEYED JESUS.**

☐ **JESUS WENT TO SLEEP.**

☐ **THE DISCIPLES WERE IN DANGER FROM THE STORM.**

☐ **JESUS ASKED, "WHERE IS YOUR FAITH?"**

☐ **THE DISCIPLES WOKE JESUS.**

☐ **A TERRIBLE WINDSTORM CAME UP.**

☐ **THE WIND STOPPED AND THE WAVES CALMED.**

Now, draw the lines from sentence #1 above in box #1. Keep going across the grid, drawing in other boxes using the order of the Bible story.

1	2	3
4	5	6
7	8	9

CAN YOU DO IT?

Encoded above each camp mug is a way to grow closer to God, but all the codes are different. Break each code and write your answer below or beside it.

QSBZ

18-5-12-25
15-14
7-15-4

TOY
BATH
IDEA
UNDER
KICKER

23-12-13-7
4-12-9-9-2

IGVE
HTNASK

HINT:
- ALPHABET/NUMBER CODE
- LETTER BEFORE CODE
- SCRAMBLED WORDS
- BACKWARD ALPHABET CODE
- RED-LETTER ACROSTIC

DIG DEEPER!

The Bible records three different accounts of Jesus calming the storm. Look at each account. Make notes on the chart about what you read in each one.

	MATTHEW 8:23-27	MARK 4:36-41	LUKE 8:22-25
WHO IS LISTED?			
WHERE WERE THEY?			
WHAT TROUBLE HAPPENED?			
WHAT DID JESUS DO OR SAY?			

QUERIES FOR THE QUEST

Query is another word for question. God asks us questions and listens to our questions to draw us closer to Him. These pages will guide you to use your Bible, to think about questions you have for God or ones He may have for you, and to journal your thoughts and feelings.

DAILY QUERY 1

Read Matthew 8:23-27.
➤ What truths did you learn about Jesus in this passage?

_____

➤ List some words that describe Jesus in this story.

_____ _____ _____ _____

➤ Praise God that He is powerful to help you in times of danger.

DAILY QUERY 2

Read Mark 4:35-41.
➤ Sound familiar? This story is in the Book of Mark too. What is something you learned about the disciples in these verses?

_____

➤ List some times you are afraid.

_____ _____ _____ _____

➤ Pray about your fear and thank God that He is powerful to help you.

_____

DAILY QUERY 3

Read Luke 8:22-25.
➤ What was Jesus doing while the disciples began to fear the storm?

_____

➤ Why do you think Jesus had such peace?

_____

➤ Describe a time someone helped you have peace in a difficult situation?

_____

➤ Pray, asking God to help you remember to turn to Him first when you need help.

_____

DAILY QUERY 4

➤ From your Bible readings this week, do you remember whose idea it was to travel across the sea in a boat?

_____

➤ Why would Jesus sail if He knew a storm was coming?

_____

➤ Jesus sometimes allows difficult things to happen to test us so that we will trust Him more. What is a time you needed help and prayed to God?

_____

➤ Pray to God now, thanking Him for how He helps you in times of need.

_____

DAILY QUERY 5
Assess Your Quest

➤ Look back at each day's query. Think about what you learned and whether it changed how you think about God and growing closer to Him. Answer each of the following questions:

➤ What truth did I discover this week?

_____

➤ What did I learn about myself and Jesus?

_____

➤ Is there anything I realized I need to confess to God and change?

_____

The Quest & Difficult Times

CLINGING CLOSE TO GOD

Explore — to investigate, study, or analyze, to become familiar with by testing or experimenting

GOD WANTS US TO EXPLORE GOING DEEPER WITH HIM BY TRUSTING HIM THROUGH THE GOOD AND BAD THINGS IN LIFE. GOD KEEPS HIS PROMISES TO US, AND WE CAN TRUST HIM TO DO WHAT HE SAYS.

JOSEPH'S LIFE

Joseph was born to Jacob and Rachael and had 11 brothers. When Joseph was 17 years old, his job was to help his brothers care for the sheep. Jacob loved Joseph more than his other children. He gave Joseph a beautiful robe of many colors. The brothers were jealous. Joseph told his family about dreams he had where he was a ruler over them. That just made them more jealous.

One day, the brothers saw Joseph coming and planned to kill him. They threw him in a pit and considered what to do. Finally, they sold Joseph as a slave to a group on its way to Egypt. The brothers rubbed goat blood on Joseph's coat and used it to convince their father that Joseph was dead.

When Joseph got to Egypt, he was sold as a slave to Potiphar, the captain of Pharaoh's guard. God was with Joseph and made everything he did successful. Soon Joseph was in charge of everything Potiphar owned. However, Potiphar's wife told him a terrible lie about Joseph. Potiphar was so angry, he had Joseph thrown in jail.

God was with Joseph in the jail. He caused the jailer to like Joseph. Soon Joseph was in charge of all the prisoners in the jail. One day two men in the jail had dreams that Joseph explained for them. Later one of the men remembered that Joseph could tell about dreams. He told Pharaoh about Joseph and Joseph was called to Pharaoh's court.

With God's help, Joseph successfully told Pharaoh about his dream and the coming famine. Pharaoh put Joseph in charge of everything in Egypt so that his country could survive the famine that was to come. Pharaoh made Joseph second in command over all of Egypt. He gave Joseph a ring, a robe, and a gold chain—symbols of the power that he was handing over to Joseph.

The famine spread all the way back to Joseph's home in Canaan. His father Jacob sent ten of the brothers to Egypt to get food. They had no idea they would be asking Joseph for what they needed! Joseph recognized his brothers, but they didn't recognize him. Joseph tested them and found they had become trustworthy men. When he told them who he was, he invited them to bring the whole family to live in Egypt where he could be sure they had food.

The whole family moved to Egypt. Jacob and Joseph were so glad to see each other again and rejoiced that God provided for them. After many years, Jacob died. Joseph's brothers worried that Joseph would harm them in revenge for what they had done to him. Instead, Joseph said, "Don't be afraid. You planned evil for me, but God planned it for good. See the survival of so many people! Don't be afraid. I will take care of you."

—based on Genesis 37–50

DIG DEEPER!

Which book of the Bible do you think contains the most questions? Go on, take a guess. If you guessed the book between Esther and Psalms, you would be right! In fact, that book has a lot more questions than other Bible books. The number of questions in Job is about **329**, while the next closest book, Jeremiah, has about **195 questions** in it.

The Gospels have quite a few questions in them also. Add these up to see how many questions are in the four Gospels:

Matthew: 177
Mark: 121
Luke: 165
John: + 167
               Total =

That's a lot of questions! Read these verses from Job and decide which question interests you the most: **Job 2:10; Job 6:11; Job 38:3; Job 38:36**.

Job wanted to know why he suffered since he was a good man. God answered him, but instead of telling Job why he suffered, God told of His own power and wisdom.

ON THE 8'S!

Practice your math skills as you figure out the words to complete each octagon. Each letter is represented by a math fact. You will need to multiply the 8's in order to figure out the missing letters.

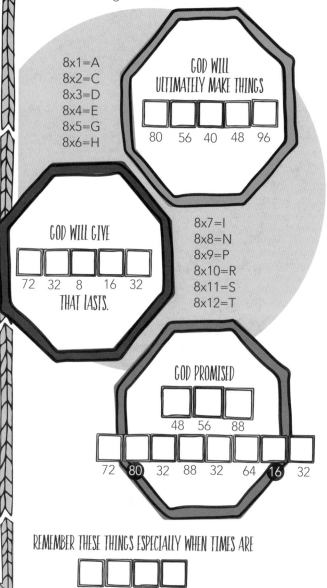

8x1=A
8x2=C
8x3=D
8x4=E
8x5=G
8x6=H

GOD WILL ULTIMATELY MAKE THINGS

80   56   40   48   96

8x7=I
8x8=N
8x9=P
8x10=R
8x11=S
8x12=T

GOD WILL GIVE

72   32   8   16   32

THAT LASTS.

GOD PROMISED

48   56   88

72   80   32   88   32   64   16   32

REMEMBER THESE THINGS ESPECIALLY WHEN TIMES ARE

48   8   80   24

DROP, DO, TELL

Put the page on the floor as flat as you can. Stand near the paper, hold your hand about waist high, and drop a paper clip onto the first box. Where the clip lands indicates what you will tell. BUT, before you tell…drop a paper clip onto the second box. That box will indicate how you will do the telling.

QUERIES FOR THE QUEST

There are no right and wrong words for writing your thoughts and feelings. If you are concerned about putting them on paper, you can write in code or use initials to represent some words. Remember, these pages are for you and God only.

DAILY QUERY 1

➤ Read Genesis 37:3-11. What do you learn about Joseph? About his father? About his brothers?

Joseph:
Joseph's father, Isaac:
Joseph's brothers:

➤ What might you have done in the same situation?_____
_____

➤ Write down the name of someone to pray for in your family.
_____

➤ Pray, asking God to help your live to honor Him.
_____

DAILY QUERY 2

➤ Read Genesis 37:17-24. Why did Joseph's brothers do this terrible thing to Joseph?_____

➤ How do you think Joseph felt? _____
_____

➤ Do you believe God was with Joseph in the pit?_____
_____

➤ Pray, thanking God for being with you even in difficult times.
_____

DAILY QUERY 3

Read Genesis 37:25-28. Some people joke about selling a sibling, but Joseph's brothers really did it. In fact, his brother Judah's actions probably saved Joseph's life. They thought he was gone, but God was preparing a future for him they could not imagine.

➤ What do you learn about the brothers, especially Judah?_____
_____

➤ Have you ever had a situation that seemed hopeless, but you saw later that God was still there taking care of you? _____
_____

➤ Pray, thanking God for how He cares for you even when it feels like you are all alone.

DAILY QUERY 4

Read Genesis 37:29-36.
➤ What do Reuben's and Jacob's reactions tell you about how upset they were to find Joseph gone? _____
_____

➤ Do you have a brother or sister you disagree with sometimes but you still love?_____

➤ How might Joseph have felt as he ended up sold to an Egyptian as a slave? _____

➤ One day Joseph would meet his brothers again and tell them, "You planned evil against me; God planned it for good." Praise God that He brings about good things out of terrible situations!

DAILY QUERY 5

Read Genesis 39:23b: "The LORD was with him (Joseph), and the LORD made everything that he did successful."
➤ How did God bless Joseph in a way that was not expected?

_____

Assess Your Quest
➤ Look back at each day's query. Think about what you learned and whether it changed how you think about God and growing closer to Him. Answer each of the following questions:

➤ What truth did I discover this week?

_____

➤ What did I learn about myself and Jesus?

_____

➤ Is there anything I realized I need to confess to God and change?

_____

The Quest & Others

GROWING CLOSER TO GOD THROUGH SERVICE

Inquire —
to ask about, to search into,
to make investigation

GOD WANTS US TO ASK HIM QUESTIONS.
IT SHOWS WE WANT TO KNOW AND
UNDERSTAND HIM MORE AND ARE SEEKING
TO FIND ANSWERS. GOD ASKS US
QUESTIONS TO DRAW US CLOSER TO HIM.

BREAKFAST WITH JESUS

Jesus asked Peter, "Do you love Me more than these?"

Peter answered, "Yes Lord. You know I love You."

"Feed my lambs," Jesus said.

Again Jesus asked Peter, "Son of John, do you love Me?"

"You know I love You," Peter answered.

"Take care of My sheep," Jesus said.

"Simon, do you love Me?" Jesus asked.

Peter was hurt that Jesus asked him this question a third time. "You know everything, Lord," he said. "You know I love You."

"Feed My sheep. When you were young, you took care of yourself. When you are old, you will need help to take care of yourself."

Jesus wanted Peter to know how he would glorify God. Then Jesus said, "Follow Me."

When Peter looked around and saw John following them, he asked Jesus, "What about him?"

Jesus said, "If I want him to live until I come back, what is that to you. You follow Me."

Jesus didn't say that John would live that long. He just meant that it was not Peter's business.

John wrote that Jesus did so many things that if they were written down, the world could not hold them all!

—based on John 21:15-25

BLOCK OUT!

Follow the directions below to discover an important word for people who want to grow closer to God.

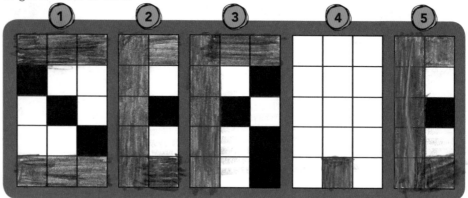

1. Shade in **all the blocks** on the **left** columns of **boxes 2 and 3**.
2. Shade in the **top blocks** of **boxes 1, 2, and 3**.
3. Shade in the **bottom blocks** of **boxes 1 and 2**.
4. Copy **box 2** onto **box 5**.
5. Shade in the **middle block** on the bottom row of **box 4**.
6. Shade in the **top 4 blocks** on the left side of **box 4**.
7. Shade in the **top 4 blocks** on the right side of **box 4**.

WHAT WORD DO YOU SEE SPELLED OUT?

Read the statements hidden in the woods. Circle the ones that you can do to practice the word you discovered above.

PRAY SILENTLY FOR SOMEONE YOU SEE.
PICK UP TRASH IN YOUR NEIGHBORHOOD.
GIVE AWAY TOYS YOU'VE OUTGROWN.
GO CAROLING.
RETURN A SHOPPING CART FOR SOMEONE.
OPEN A DOOR FOR SOMEONE.
PACK FOOD BOXES FOR A FOOD PANTRY.
SEND ENCOURAGING CARDS TO MISSIONARIES.
BE A FRIEND TO SOMEONE WHO NEEDS A FRIEND.

THE DOT GAME

Play this game with a partner. Take turns naming a fact from the Bible story (John 21:21-22). If you can name a fact, draw a line from one dot to another, either up and down or side to side (not diagonally). If, on your turn, you complete a square, print your initials inside the square. The winner is the player who completes the most squares.

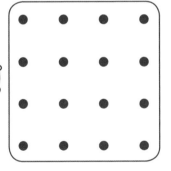

Name facts from this meeting's Bible story during each turn.

Do the same thing with a Bible story from a different meeting.

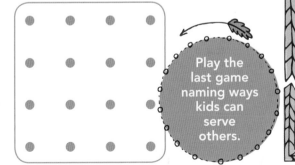

Play the last game naming ways kids can serve others.

DIG DEEPER!

Read Matthew 13:52-53. Jesus compared a student of Scripture to a rich man who gathers both new and old treasures from his storeroom.

Think about this: ANY TIME YOU HOLD A COMPLETE BIBLE, YOU HOLD BOTH NEW TREASURES AND OLD TREASURES.

Some people like to read the New Testament best. Others prefer the Old Testament. Some people love verses they learned as a child and others love to learn about verses they've never considered before. The good news is that they are all yours.

Think about Bible verses you have learned. Repeat one of them back to God and thank Him for it. (Remember that you have learned Matthew 7:7-11 during this study!)

Holding your Bible, thank God for giving you both new and old treasures in His Word.

QUERIES FOR THE QUEST

Query is another word for question. God asks us questions and listens to our questions to draw us closer to Him. These pages will guide you to use your Bible, to think about questions you have for God or ones He may have for you, and to journal your thoughts and feelings.

DAILY QUERY 1

➤ Read John 21:3-6. What did you learn about Jesus?_____
_____

➤ Why do you think the disciples did not realize Jesus was the One standing on the shore?_____
_____

➤ What might you have done in the same situation?_____
_____

➤ Pray, asking God to make it clear to you when He is speaking to you.

_____

DAILY QUERY 2

Read John 21:7-11.

➤ What do you notice about what Jesus says to the disciples? _____
_____

➤ How might Peter and John have felt? _____
_____

➤ Why did Peter jump out of the boat? Would you have done the same thing? _____

➤ What does this tell you about yourself? _____
_____

➤ Pray, asking God to help you have boldness and confidence in knowing Him.

DAILY QUERY 3

Read John 21:12-14.
➤ What do you learn about the disciples from this passage? _____
_____

➤ Why do you think Jesus appeared to the disciples multiple times? _____
_____

➤ Do you think that Jesus wants people to know Him so much that He gives them many chances to get to know Him?_____
_____

➤ Pray, thanking God for seeking after you.
_____

DAILY QUERY 4

Read John 21:15-17.
➤ What do you learn about Jesus and Peter? _____
_____

➤ Why do you think Jesus asked Peter the same question three times? _____
_____

➤ How was Peter to show his love for Jesus? _____
_____

➤ How might Jesus asked you to serve Him? _____
_____

➤ Pray, asking God to show you who He wants you to serve.
_____

DAILY QUERY 5

Read John 21:18-22.

Assess Your Quest
➤ Look back at each day's query. Think about what you learned and whether it changed how you think about God and growing closer to Him. Answer each of the following questions:

➤ What truth did I discover this week?
_____

➤ What did I learn about myself and Jesus?
_____

➤ Is there anything I realized I need to confess to God and change?
_____

The Quest & Promise

GOD WILL GO WITH US TO THE END

Examine — to inspect closely, to test the condition of, to inquire into carefully

LIFE HAS A WAY OF TESTING US. GOD WANTS US TO EXAMINE EVERY CIRCUMSTANCE IN LIFE, SEE HIS PLAN FOR US, AND SEEK HOW HE WANTS US TO OBEY HIM.

DAVID WAS ANOINTED AND FOUGHT GOLIATH

Saul was not going to be king of Israel anymore. He had disobeyed God. Israel needed a new king, a better king. God told Samuel to visit a man in Bethlehem named Jesse. Jesse had eight sons, and one of them would be Israel's king. Samuel did what God told him to do. He went to Bethlehem to meet with Jesse and his sons. Jesse's oldest son, Eliab, was tall and handsome.

"This must be the one God chose to be king," Samuel thought. "Samuel, he's not the one," God said. "Do not pay attention to what he looks like. You look at what you can see on the outside, but I see the heart." One by one, Jesse's sons approached Samuel, but God had not chosen any of them. "Do you have any more sons?" Samuel asked. "Yes," Jesse said. "My youngest son, David, is in the field taking care of the sheep." Jesse sent for David. When David arrived, God told Samuel, "He's the one!"

Samuel poured oil on David's head, and the Spirit of the Lord was with David. Then Samuel went back home. The Spirit of the Lord was not with Saul anymore. In fact, Saul was bothered by an evil spirit. Saul's servants suggested Saul find someone who could play the harp. Hearing beautiful music might make Saul feel better when the evil spirit bothered him. One of Saul's officials knew just the person to play the harp—David, son of Jesse. David came to Saul and whenever Saul felt troubled, David played his harp, and Saul felt better.

At this time, Israel's enemies, the Philistines, got ready for war. They were going to attack a town in Judah. King Saul got his army ready to fight. The Israelites camped on one hill while the Philistines camped on another. There was a valley between them. The Philistines had a great warrior named Goliath. At 9 feet 9 inches tall, Goliath was their hero. Goliath shouted at the Israelites, "Why are you lined up, ready for battle? Send me your best man, and we'll fight one-on-one." But none of the Israelites wanted to fight Goliath. They were afraid of him.

Jesse's three oldest sons were part of the Israelite army camped on a hill. Jesse sent David to check on his brothers and to give them something to eat. David saw Goliath and watched the Israelites run away in fear. David heard that Saul had offered a great reward to the man who killed Goliath. David volunteered to fight. "You don't stand a chance against Goliath," Saul argued. "I have killed wild animals," David explained. "God will keep me safe." Saul allowed David to fight Goliath. He offered his armor to David, but David could hardly move. He took off the armor and chose five smooth stones from a nearby stream. David was armed only with the stones and a slingshot. Goliath saw David and made fun of him because he was just a boy. "You come to fight with a spear and sword," David replied, "but I come to fight in the name of God! You have insulted Him, and God always wins His battles!" David ran toward Goliath. He slung a rock at Goliath, and the rock hit Goliath in the forehead. Goliath fell facedown, and David killed him without even having a sword.

-based on 1 Samuel 16-17

BLOCK LETTERS

Fill in the answers to the clues. Then fill in the blanks in the sentence, using the letters in the clues. Find the answer to the question: What do I need for my quest?

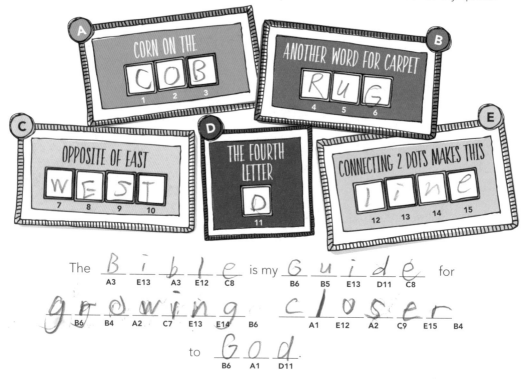

A — CORN ON THE
C O B
1 2 3

B — ANOTHER WORD FOR CARPET
R U G
4 5 6

C — OPPOSITE OF EAST
W E S T
7 8 9 10

D — THE FOURTH LETTER
D
11

E — CONNECTING 2 DOTS MAKES THIS
l i n e
12 13 14 15

The B i b l e is my G u i d e for
   A3 E13 A3 E12 C8   B6 B5 E13 D11 C8

g r o w i n g   c l o s e r
B6 B4 A2 C7 E13 E14 B6   A1 E12 A2 C9 E15 B4

to G o d .
  B6 A1 D11

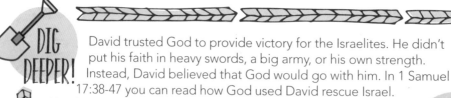

DIG DEEPER!

David trusted God to provide victory for the Israelites. He didn't put his faith in heavy swords, a big army, or his own strength. Instead, David believed that God would go with him. In 1 Samuel 17:38-47 you can read how God used David rescue Israel.

Check each statement below that is true.

___ Saul put a bronze helmet on David's head.
___ David put 5 smooth stones in his shepherd's bag.
___ David faced Goliath with only a sling in his hand.
___ When Goliath saw David he laughed at him.
___ Goliath came to fight David with a sword, spear, and javelin.
___ David came to fight Goliath in the name of the LORD of Armies.
___ David believed that the battle belonged to the LORD.

DID YOU FIND SIX CORRECT STATEMENTS?

CHEW CAN REED ITT!

Could you read the title? If not, try slurring the words together. Got it? Now, try to read these questions. Then answer them!

VAT DOZ GOD DOOTOO ELPU?

VATIS YOAR PHAV O ARET VERS?

HOWL ONG ILLUR KWEST BEE?

HOO ILL BEE WITCHEW FOR EHVR?

A SAILING QUEST

Play this game with a friend or alone. Use a small item as your sailboat. How to play:

➤ You must sail to each island.

➤ To move your boat, you must answer a question, tell a way to grow closer to God, or repeat any verse from Matthew 7:7-11.

➤ Move your boat across three lines of waves if you answer a review question, across two lines of waves if you tell a way to grow closer to God, or across one line of waves if you repeat a memory verse.

➤ If you play the game with a friend, the first player to reach all three islands is the winner. If you play alone, try to reach each island with the fewest waves possible.

QUERIES FOR THE QUEST

Although these are the last pages in your book, you can continue your queries with God. Grab a notebook, a pen or pencil, and your Bible. Keep them where you are reminded to use them each day. Choose a book of the Bible, such as Mark, and read a few verses in that book each day. Record what you learn, how you feel, what God is teaching you, and anything else you want to include.

DAILY QUERY 1

Read Psalm 119:97-100.
➤ What do you learn about God's Word?

_____

➤ How do these Bible verses make you feel?_____

_____

➤ In what ways might you be wise and understanding if you study and obey God's Word?

_____

➤ Pray, asking God to show you the way He wants you to live.

_____

DAILY QUERY 2

Read Psalm 119:111-112.
➤ How long will God's Word lead you?

_____

➤ What about the Bible makes you feel joy?

_____

➤ What does God want you to learn from these verses?

_____

➤ Pray, asking God to help you study the Bible regularly.

_____

DAILY QUERY 3

Read Psalm 119:129-132.
➤ What are two of God's commands, decrees, or statutes you find wonderful?

_____

➤ Why might King David have thought God's laws are wonderful?

_____

➤ What does God want you to learn from these verses?

_____

➤ Pray, thanking God for teaching you through the Bible.

_____

DAILY QUERY 4

Read Psalm 119:133-136.
➤ How might sin rule a person's life?

_____

➤ How can the Bible help a person stay away from sin ruling his life?

_____

➤ What examples can you recall of people following God's instructions and help them stop making bad choices?

_____

➤ Pray, asking God for forgiveness of your sins.

_____

DAILY QUERY 5

Read Psalm 119:171-173.
➤ What do you want to praise God for doing or being?

_____

➤ What promises has God made? Is He keeping those promises?

_____

➤ Write down all the words in these verses that mean God's Word. How do you feel about their being so many?

_____

THE QUEST: GROWING CLOSER TO GOD IS OUR QUEST

This week we are focusing on people as God's prized creation, made in His image. Despite the rebellion of sin, because of God's great love for us, He made a plan to rescue us by sending His Son, Jesus.

KEY VERSE: "Ask, and it will be given to you. Seek, and you will find. Knock, and the door will be opened to you." Matthew 7:7

BIBLE STORY PASSAGE:
Genesis 1–3

TEACHING POINTS

➤ Talk about a quest. The Quest for Kids is about the adventure (quest) of knowing God more.

➤ Review Genesis 1–3. Emphasize people are God's prized creation. He created us in His image, declared us very good, and desires to have a lasting relationship with us. Despite the rebellion of sin, because of God's great love for us, He made a plan to rescue us by sending His Son, Jesus. God desires to bring us back into a restored relationship with Him, so that we know God, grow closer to Him, and walk with Him day by day.

➤ Talk about how asking questions is one important way we learn about the world around us. God wants us to ask Him questions. It shows we want to know and understand Him more.

BIBLE STORY

Read today's Bible story about Adam and Eve in Genesis 1–3. Ask the following review questions:
Q1: How did God create everything?
A1: He spoke everything into existence. (Genesis 1)

Q2: How did God describe everything He created?
A2: God said, "It is good." (Genesis 1)
Q3: How are man and woman special?
A3: Man and woman are created in the image of God. (Genesis 1:27)
Q4: How did the serpent trick Eve?
A4: Told her the fruit would make her like God (Genesis 3:3)
Q6: After Adam and Eve ate, what did they do when they heard God?
A6: They hid in the garden. (Genesis 3:8)
Q7: What question did God ask Adam after Adam hid?
A7: Where are you? (Genesis 3:9)
Q8: What hope did God give Adam and Eve?
A8: God promised that He would send a Savior, and God clothed them. (Genesis 3:15,21)

GO DEEPER

Q9: What words can you use to describe God?
A9: Loving, forgiving, Creator, etc.

PRAY AND JOURNAL

➤ Complete pages 10-11 together.

ACTIVITY

➤ Use sheets of paper to make a path. Each time your child tells a fact about today's Bible story, she advances two spaces. Let your child create questions for you to answer about the Bible story.

THE QUEST AND FAITH: FOLLOWING GOD'S PLAN

This week we are focusing on following God's leading, whether anything is too hard for God, and the ultimate promise that God will right every wrong at some time. The gospel will be presented to kids after discussing Abraham's faith.

KEY VERSE: "For everyone who asks receives, and the one who seeks finds, and to the one who knocks, the door will be opened." Matthew 7:8

BIBLE STORY PASSAGE:
Genesis 12:1-5 and 15:1-6

TEACHING POINTS

➤ Growing closer to God is a quest that lasts a lifetime.

➤ God planned each person's journey before the person was ever born.

➤ God sent His Son Jesus to be the Savior and bring people back to Himself.

➤ Today we will learn how Abraham spent his life growing closer to God.

BIBLE STORY
Abraham's story takes up several chapters in Genesis. Read together Genesis 12:1-5 and 15:1-6 to find ways Abraham obeyed God. Ask the following review questions:
Q1: Where did God tell Abram to go?
A1: To a land He would show Abram (Gen.12:1)
Q2: Who did Abram take with him?
A2: Sarai, Lot, and his servants (Gen. 12:5)
Q3: How many children did God promise to Abram?
A2: More than the stars in the sky (Gen. 15:3)
Q4: How did Abram respond to God's promise?

A4: He believed what God said (Gen. 15:6)

GO DEEPER
Q5: What do you think God wants us to learn from the story of Abram?
A5: God is pleased when people obey Him. God can do anything.
Q6: What kinds of plans might God have for your life?

PRAY AND JOURNAL

➤ Complete pages 16-17 together as you pray and write about what God is teaching you.

ACTIVITY
Make a GCTGTM (Growing Closer to God Text Message) Shelf Minder:

➤ Form a body shape from chenille stems.

➤ Abbreviate a message about growing closer to God to be like a text message (such as LOL for laughing out loud). Write it on a small rectangle of paper.

➤ Tape the message to one hand of the body shape.

➤ Place the shelf minder on a book shelf, a table, or other flat surface in your home.

THE QUEST AND FEAR: TRUSTING AND DEPENDING ON GOD

This week focuses on trusting and depending on God during times of fear. Jesus has power over anything we might fear and over all creation. Kids can learn that Jesus is stronger than anything that might be standing in their way of trusting God.

KEY VERSE: "Who among you, if his son asks him for bread, will give him a stone?" Matthew 7:9

BIBLE STORY PASSAGE:
Matthew 8:23-27

TEACHING POINTS
➤ Read Matthew 8:26 together to introduce the question Jesus asked the disciples.

➤ Talk together about times you are afraid and how you can trust God to care for you.

➤ Continue on the quest to learn more about trusting and depending on God.

BIBLE STORY
Read about the disciples on the lake in Matthew 8:23-27. Ask the following review questions:
Q1: What was happening to the boat?
A1: It was sinking (Matthew 8:24)
Q1: What was Jesus doing during the storm?
A2: Sleeping! (Matthew 8:24)
Q3: What did Jesus do to the storm?
A3: Made it stop (Matthew 8:26)
Q4: How did the disciples feel?
A4: Amazed (Matthew 8:27)

GO DEEPER
Q5: What do you think God wants us to learn from the story of the disciples and the storm?
A5: Jesus is in control of everything and we have no need to fear.
Q6: Why might God not always take what we fear away?
A6: To help us learn to trust Him as we go through the fear and to remember His presence at all times.

PRAY AND JOURNAL
➤ Complete pages 22-23 together as you pray and write about what God is teaching you.

ACTIVITY
Make truth spinners:
➤ Guide your child to write on the shiny side of a used CD (with a permanent marker) two or three things he might do to increase his dependence on God.

➤ Place the CD on top of a marble so that the marble pushes up slightly through the hole in the CD. Twist the marble and watch the CD spin.

➤ Time how long the CD will spin. Try to make it spin longer.

➤ Remark that the spinner is fun, but it is also a reminder that you and your child are on a lifetime quest with God, the One who is in control of everything.

THE QUEST AND DIFFICULT TIMES: CLINGING CLOSE TO GOD

This week we are focusing on what difficult times are, how God comforts people during those times, and His promise to ultimately take care of things. Kids will learn who they can go to for help.

KEY VERSE: "Or if he asks for a fish, will give him a snake?" Matthew 7:10

BIBLE STORY PASSAGE:
Various passages from Genesis 37–50

TEACHING POINTS

➤ Today we will learn how to grow closer to God even during difficult situations.

➤ Ask your child if he can think of a difficult situation in his life. Pray with him and ask God to take care of him and lead him through that difficult time.

BIBLE STORY
Read Genesis 37:12-36 about Joseph being sold into slavery.
Ask the following review questions:
Q1: Where did the brothers put Joseph?
A1: In a pit in the wilderness (Genesis 37:21)
Q2: What was Joseph wearing when his brothers trapped him?
A2: A colorful robe (Genesis 37:23)
Q3: What did Joseph's brothers do to him when they heard the caravan coming?
A3: Sold him as a slave (Genesis 37:28)

GO DEEPER
Q4: What was difficult for Joseph in this story?
A4: His brothers hated him and he was taken to a foreign country as a slave.
Q5: What do you think God wants us to learn from the Bible story?
A5: God will always be with us during hard times and will comfort us.

PRAY AND JOURNAL

➤ Complete pages 28-29 together as you pray and write about what God is teaching you.

ACTIVITY
Make "My Quest Paper Gliders"

➤ On a large paper strip, print two ways to grow closer to God. On a shorter strip, print *My Quest: Growing Closer to God.*

➤ Slide one paper clip into an end of a straw with the narrower part of the clip inside the straw. Do the same on the other end.

➤ Roll both paper strips into circles and slide them into different clips on the straw with the circles lined up one behind the other.

➤ Toss the glider and try to say the words of Matthew 7:10 before it lands.

THE QUEST AND OTHERS: GROWING CLOSER TO GOD THROUGH SERVICE

This week focuses on how Jesus is faithful to forgive and redeem us, calling us to follow Him. As we follow Him, we are called to serve Him by serving others.

KEY VERSE: "If you then, who are evil, know how to give good gifts to your children, how much more will your Father in heaven give good things to those who ask him." Matthew 7:11

BIBLE STORY PASSAGE:
John 21:15-25

TEACHING POINTS

➤ Together read Matthew 7:11 to introduce how much more God cares for people than anyone else does.

➤ Today we will learn how to grow closer to God by serving Him and others.

BIBLE STORY
Read today's Bible story about Jesus and Peter in John 21:15–25.
Ask the following review questions:
Q1: How many times did Jesus ask if Peter loved Him?
A1: 3 (John 21:15, 16, 19)
Q2: What did Jesus tell Peter three times to do?
A2: Take care of His sheep (John 21:15, 16, 17)
Q3: Who was Peter to follow?
A3: Jesus (John 21:19)

GO DEEPER
Q4: What do you think God wants us to learn from the Bible story?
A4: Even when we sin, Jesus is faithful to forgive us and call us to serve Him.
Q5: How can people serve God?
A5: By obeying Him and caring for others

PRAY AND JOURNAL

➤ Complete pages 34-35 as you pray and write about what God is teaching you.

ACTIVITY
Perform an act of service by choosing one of these activities or another of your choice.

➤ Prepare and send a care package to a soldier.

➤ Work together at a shelter to sort clothing, serve a meal, or distribute groceries.

➤ Take cold bottled water to police departments, fire stations, or first responders.

➤ Gather gently used toys and deliver them to a family shelter.

THE QUEST AND PROMISE: GOD WILL GO WITH US TO THE END

This week focuses the fact that this journey lasts a lifetime. One major way people can grow closer to God all during their lives is to study God's Word because it has wisdom for them no matter their ages or circumstances. King David recognized the importance of God's Word and worked to do all he knew to do.

KEY VERSE: Review Matthew 7:7-11

BIBLE STORY PASSAGE:
1 Samuel 16–17

TEACHING POINTS

➤ Together read Psalm 119:105 to introduce the importance of God's Word to people.

➤ Ask, "Why do you think remembering Bible verses and stories is important?"

➤ Share favorite Bible verses with each other.

➤ Today we will learn how the Bible helps us grow closer to God for our entire lives.

BIBLE STORY

Read today's Bible story from this activity book or 1 Samuel 16–17. Ask the following review questions:

Q1: Who had God chosen to be the next king of Israel?
A1: David (1 Samuel 16:12)
Q2: What instrument did David play and compose songs to God using? \
A2: A harp or lyre (1 Samuel 16:18)
Q3: How did God show He was with David?
A3: The Spirit of the Lord was on David. (1 Samuel 16:13)
Q4: What did David do in today's Bible story that showed He was willing to trust God?

A4: David fought Goliath. (1 Samuel 17)

GO DEEPER
Discussion Questions
Q4: What do you think God wants us to learn from the Bible story?
A4: God gives us direction for what to do and how to grow closer to Him.
Q5: How long does a person's quest for God continue?
Q5: For a lifetime!

PRAY AND JOURNAL

➤ Complete pages 42-43 together as you pray and write about what God is teaching you.

ACTIVITY
Create a Bible memory plan:

➤ Together print the words of these verses (or others you choose) on different index cards:
1 Corinthians 16:8; Psalm 13:10; Psalm 119:105; Ephesians 6:14; Ephesians 6:15; Ephesians 6:16; Ephesians 6:17; Ephesians 6:18; 2 Timothy 3:16; James 1:22.

➤ Cut light-weight cardboard into an easel shape. Stack the index cards and display them on the stand.

➤ Memorize the verse on the first card. Place it at the back of the stack. Choose another card the next day.

➤ Review the cards often.

Certificate of Completion

This certificate is awarded to

_____

on

_____

(date)

For completing

THE QUEST FOR KIDS: AN EXPEDITION TOWARD A DEEPER RELATIONSHIP WITH GOD

_____

(PARENT OR LEADER'S SIGNATURE)